This book belongs to :

....

A B C D E F G H I J 9 8 7

□ ☆ ⬡ △

2 3 4 5 6

KOTOKOTO
SCHOOL

Test Your Color

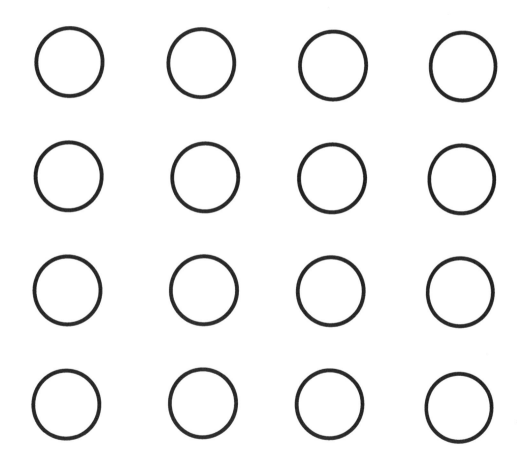

Numbers

One

Two

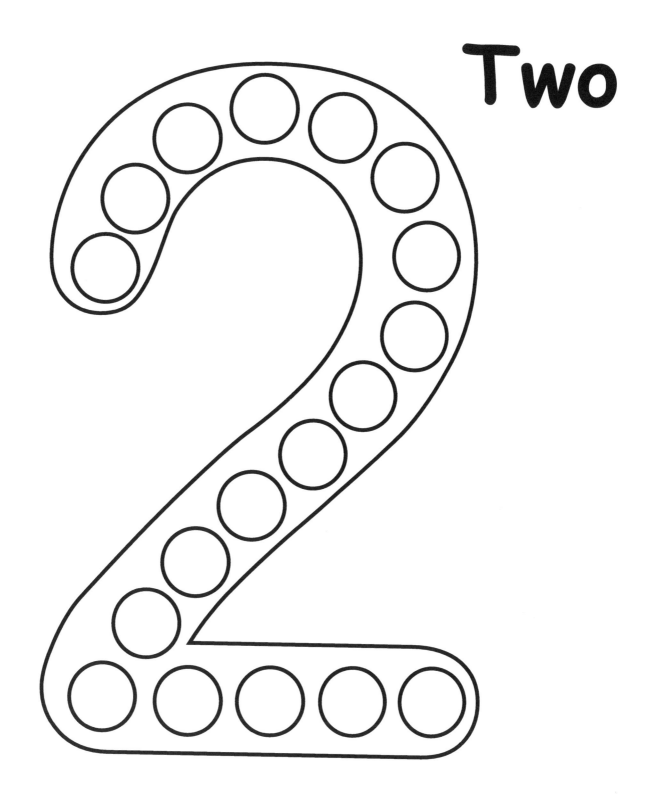

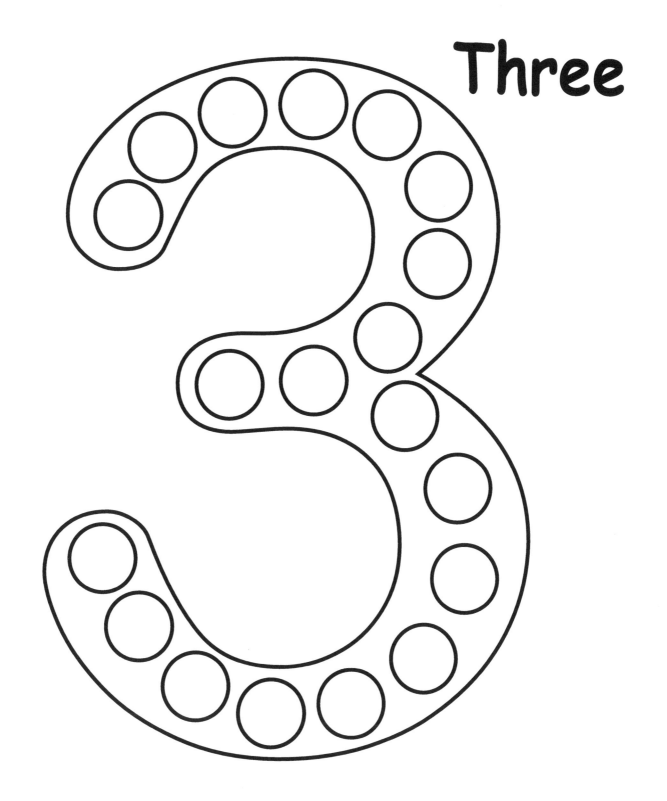

Three

Four

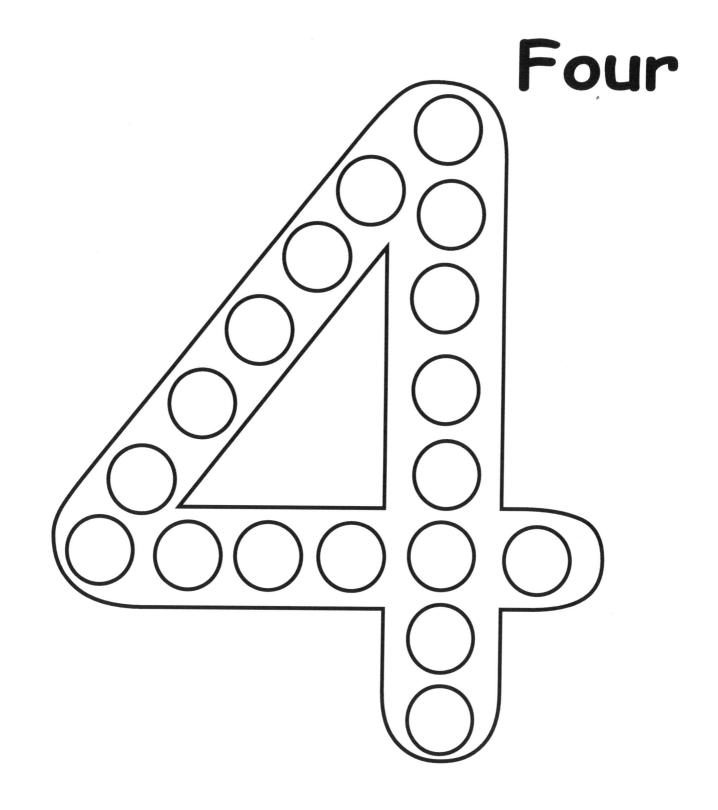

Five

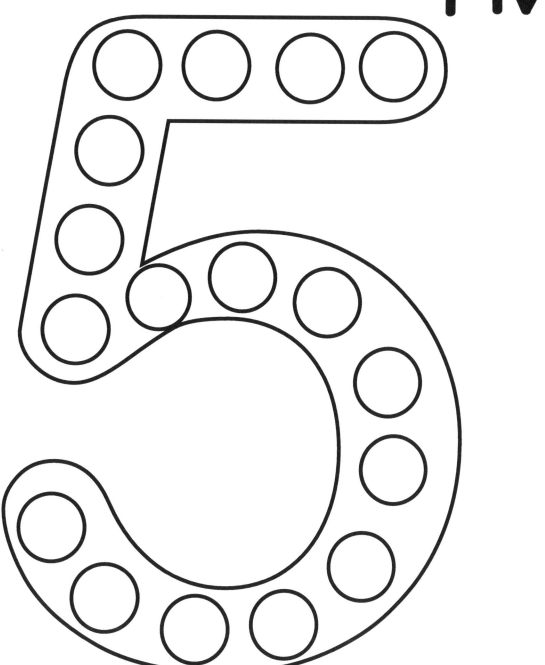

Six

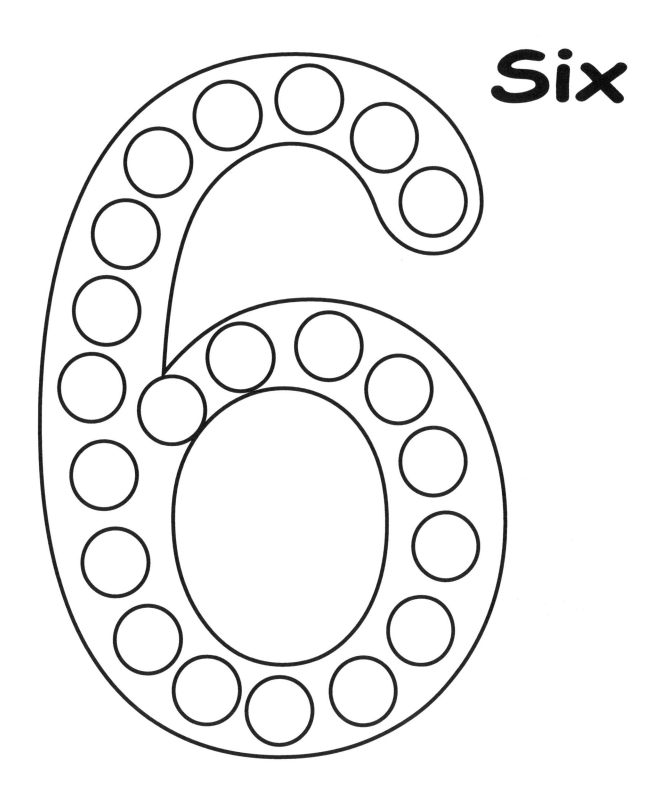

Seven

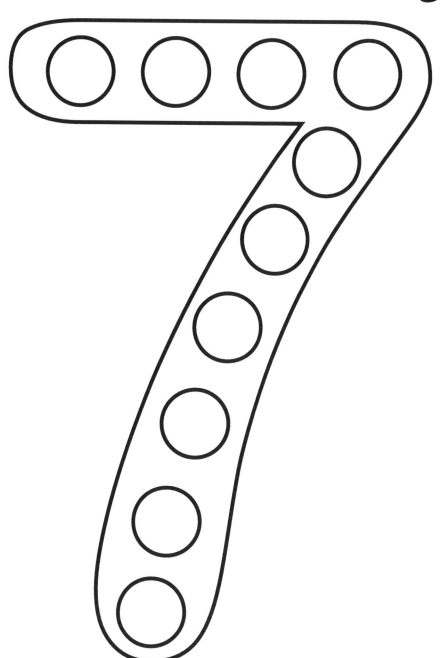

Eight

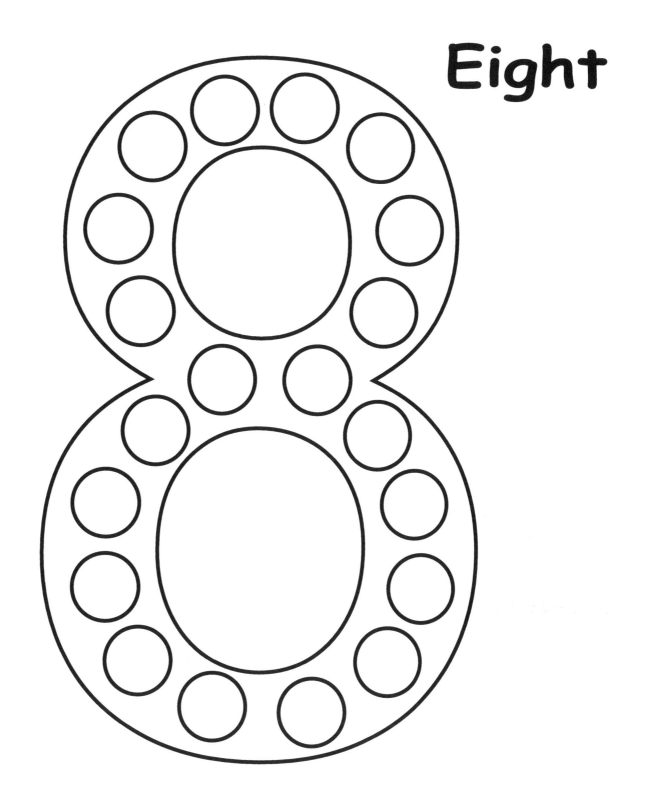

Nine

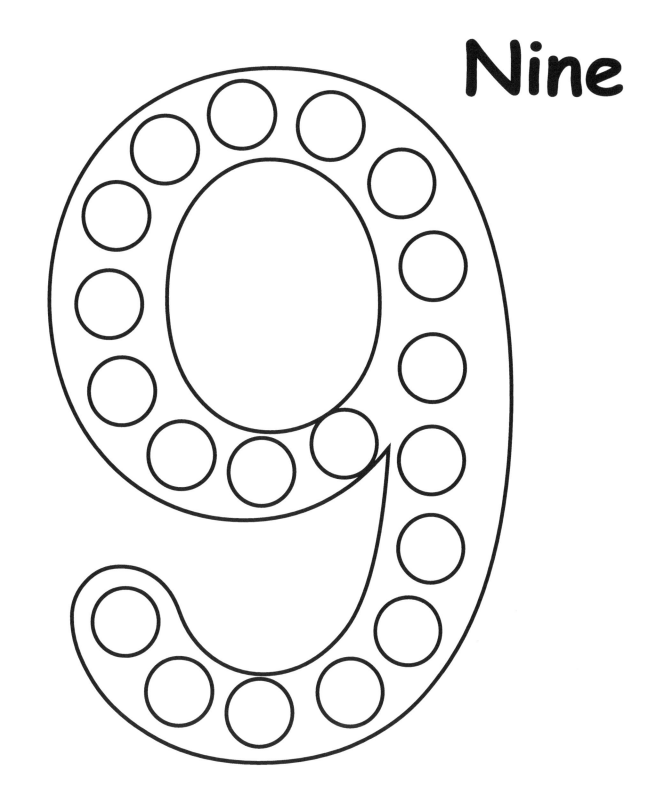

SHAPES

  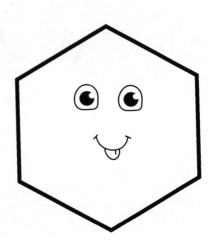

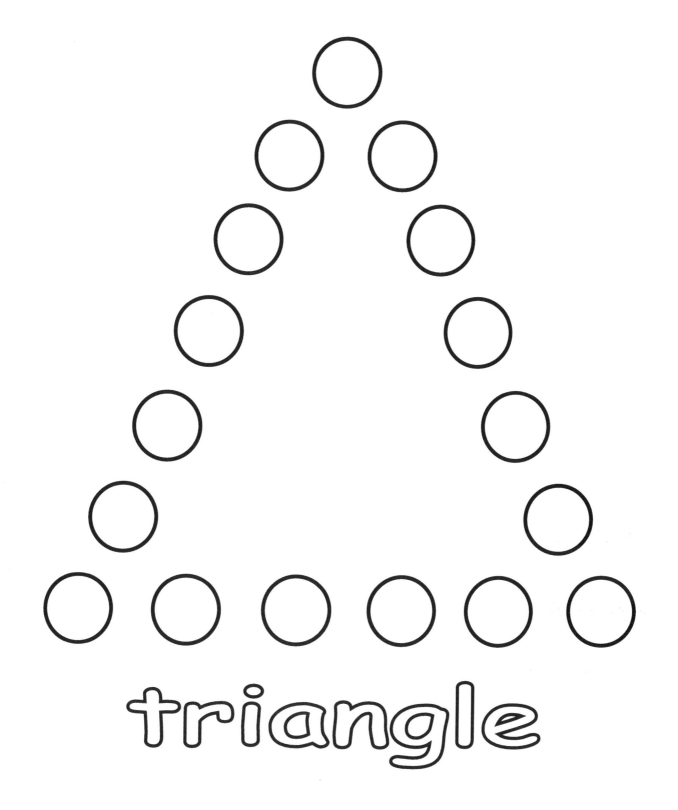

triangle

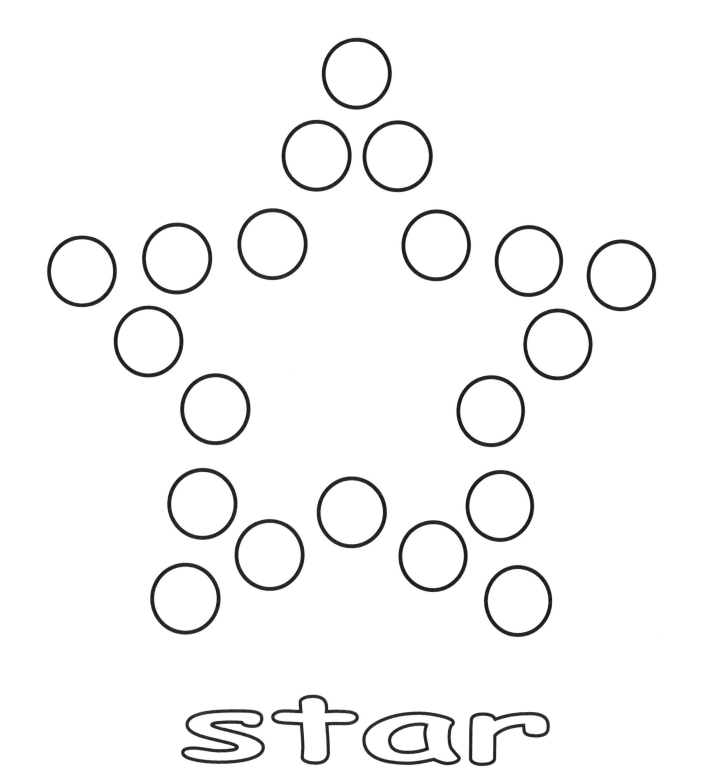

heart

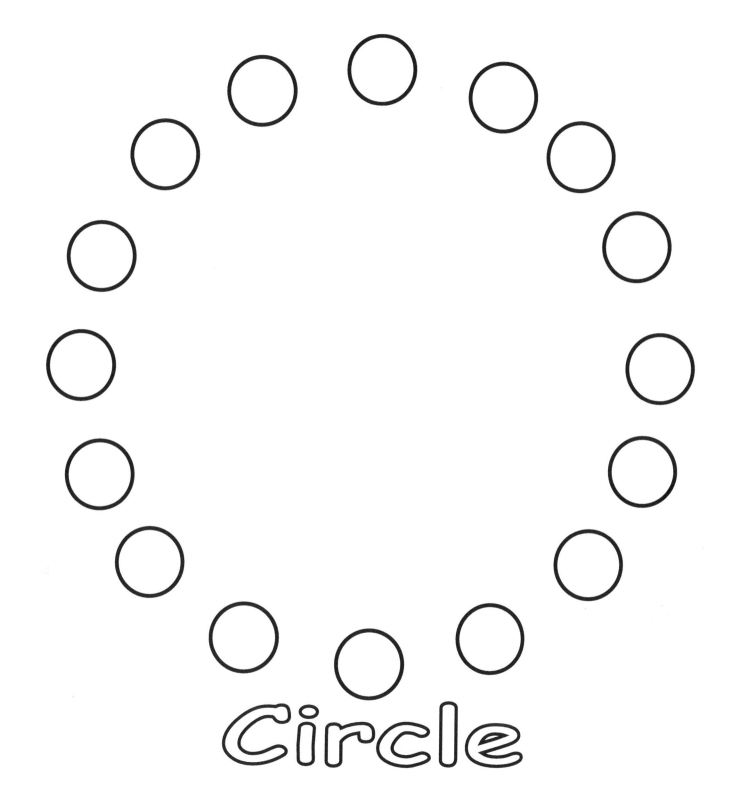

Circle

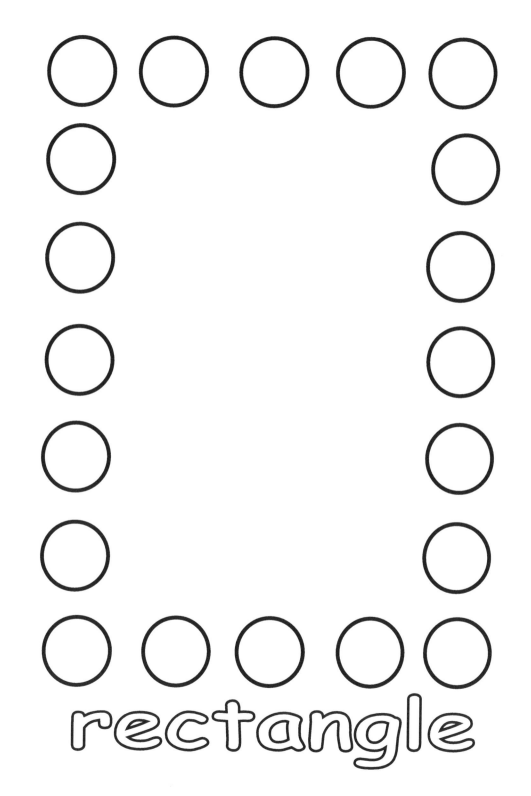

rectangle

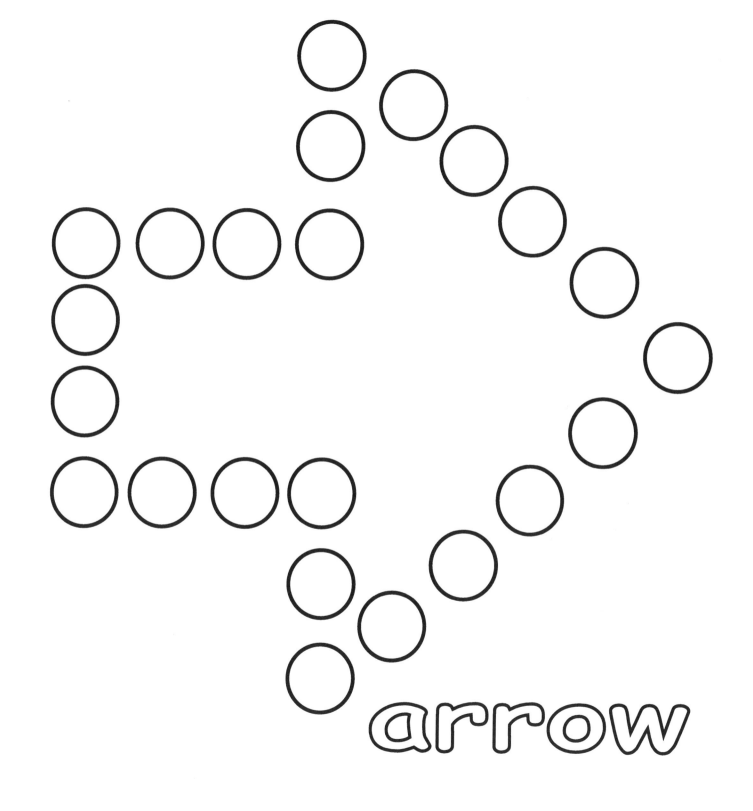

arrow

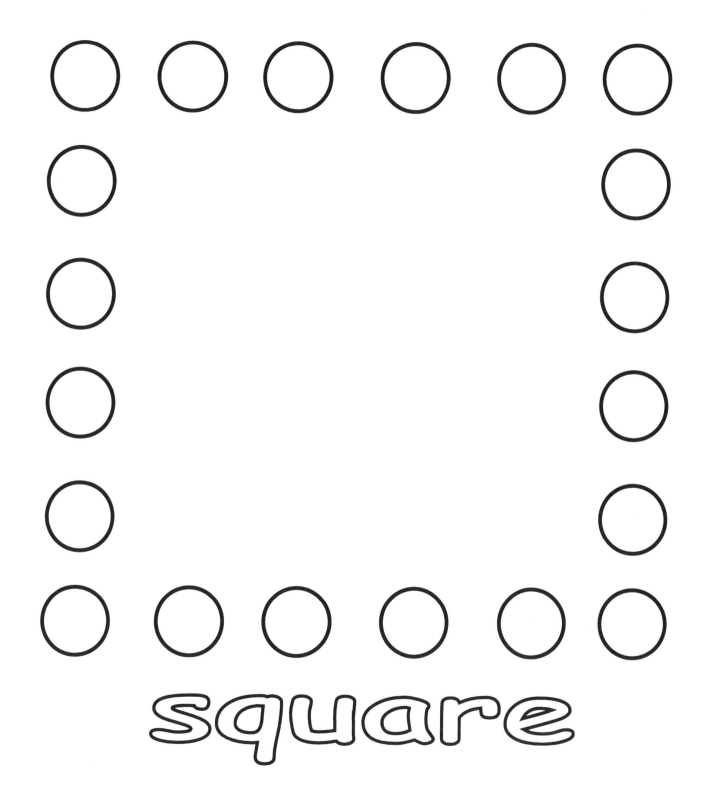

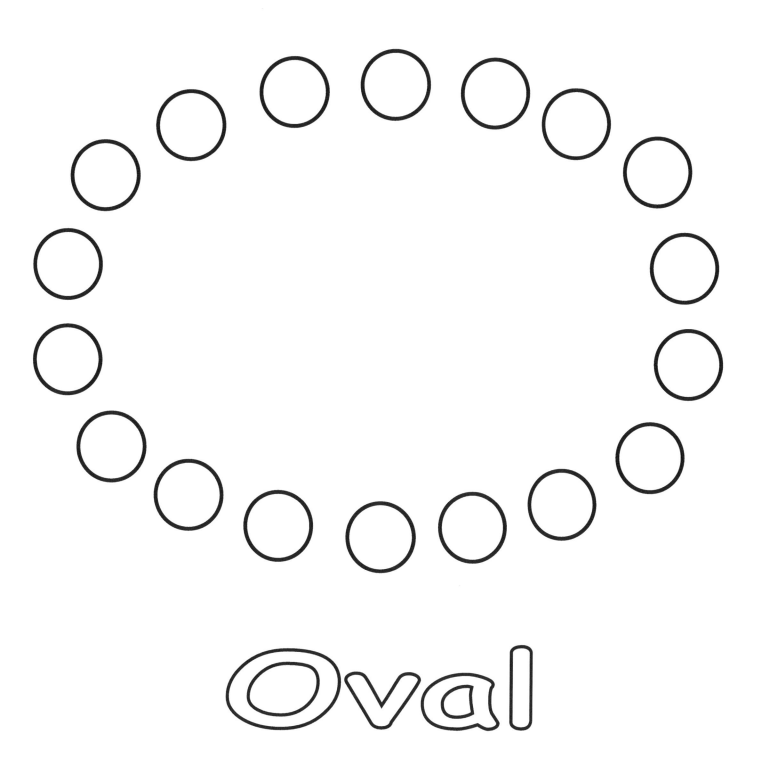

Oval

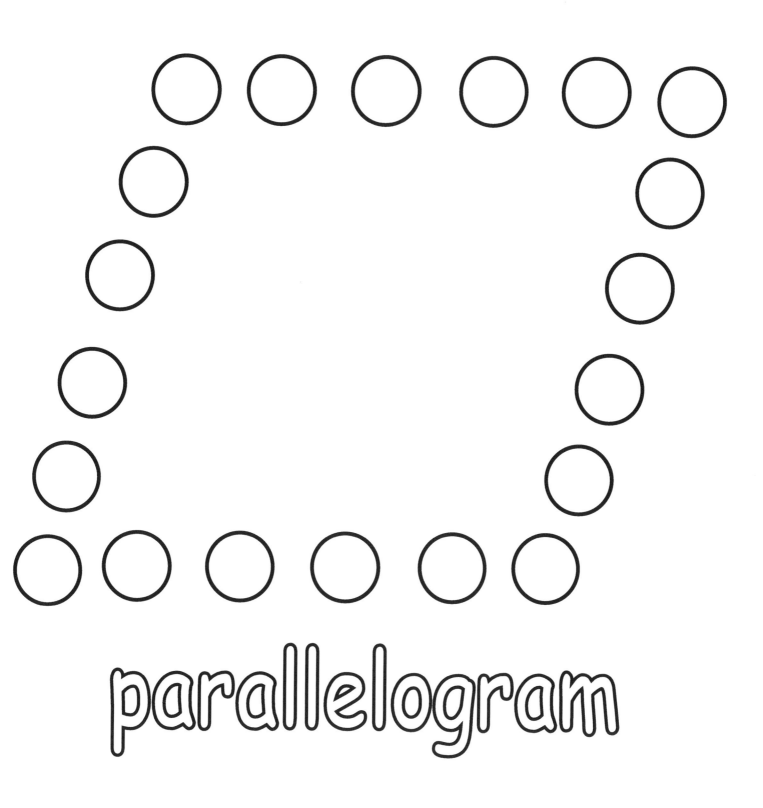

parallelogram

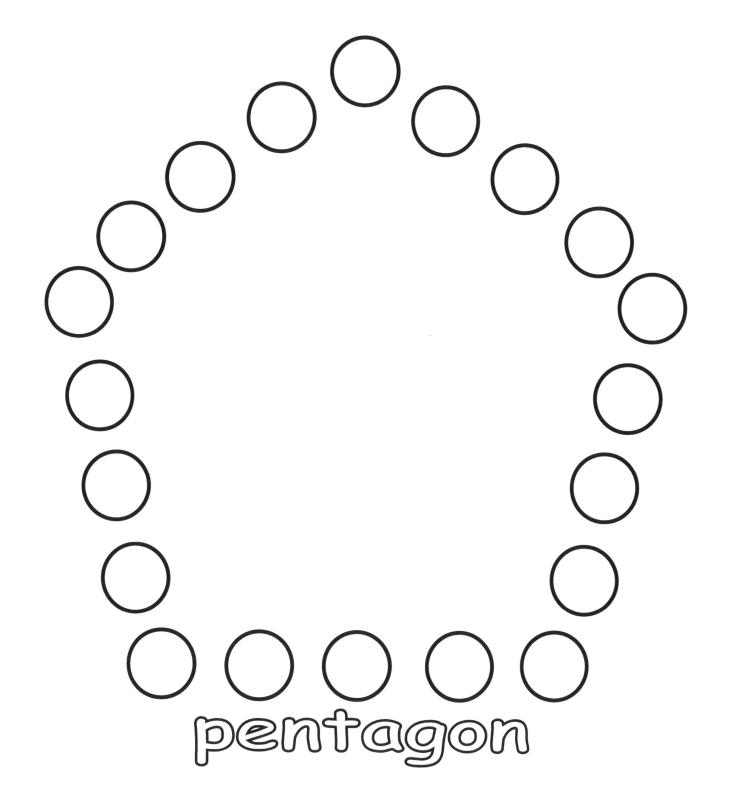

pentagon

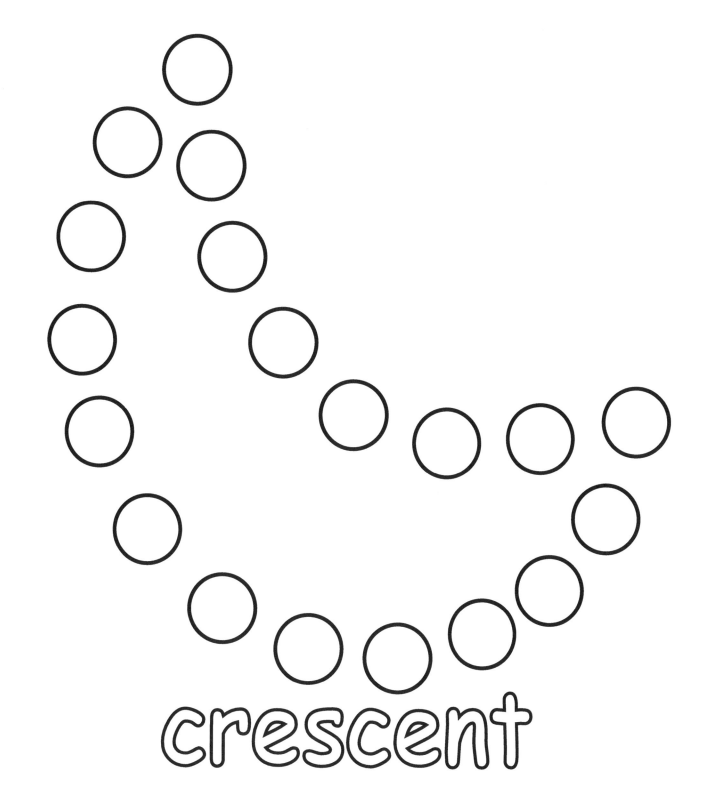

crescent

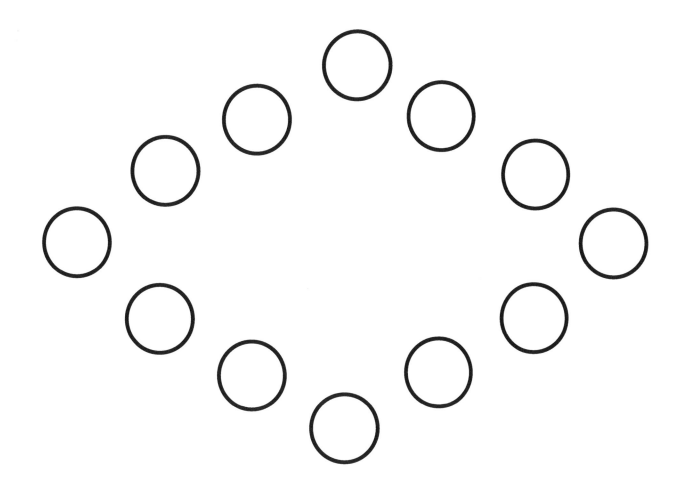

rhombus

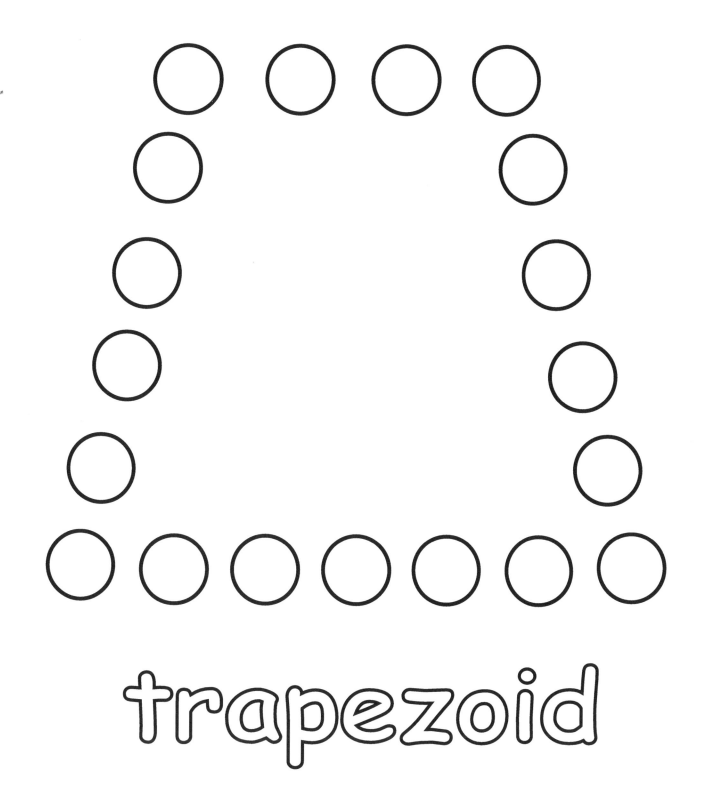

trapezoid

LETTERS

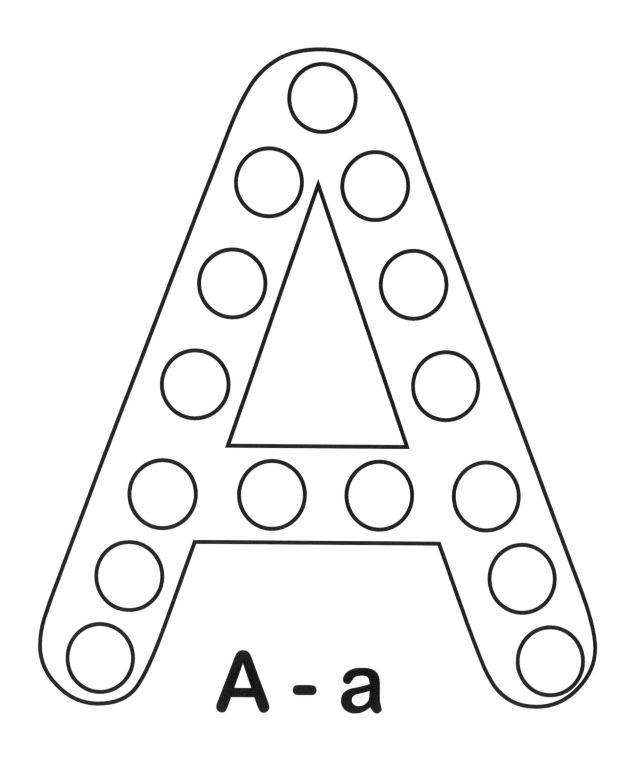

B - b

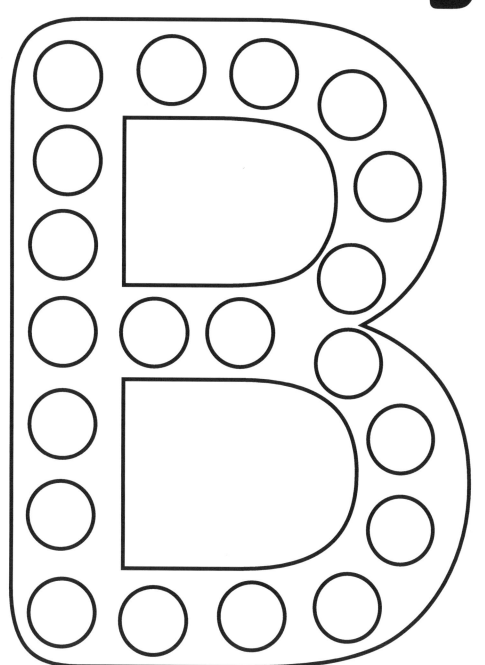

C - c

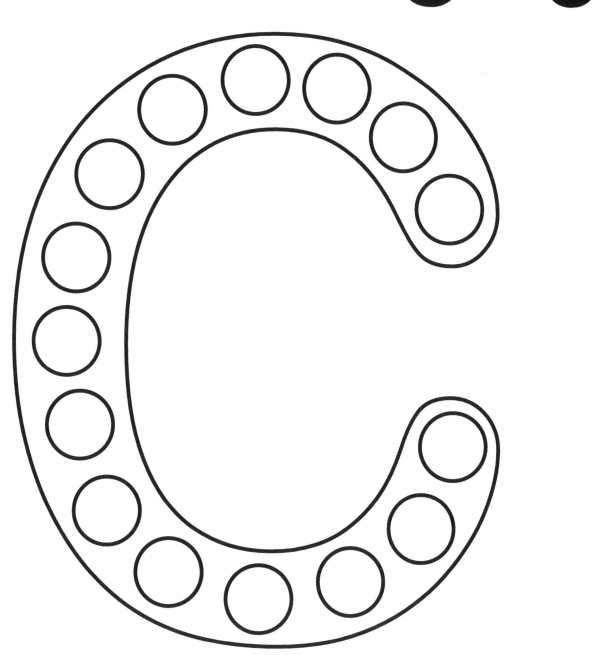

D - d

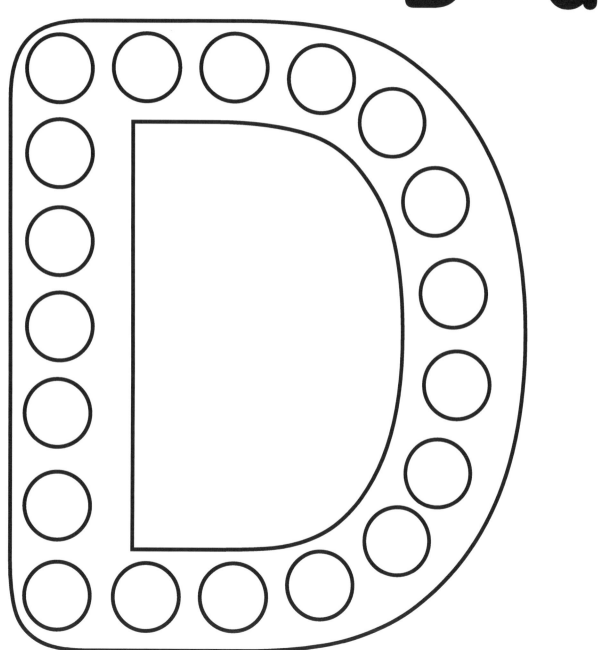

E - e

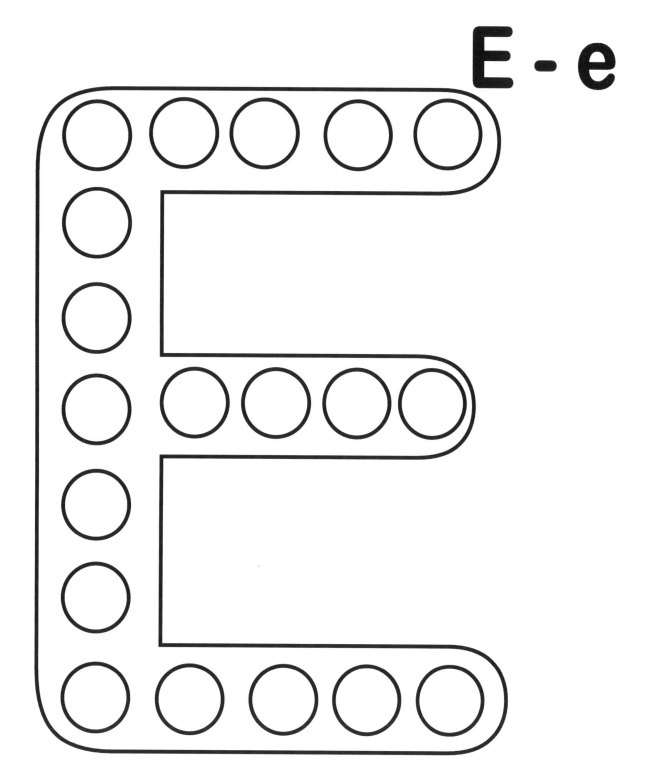

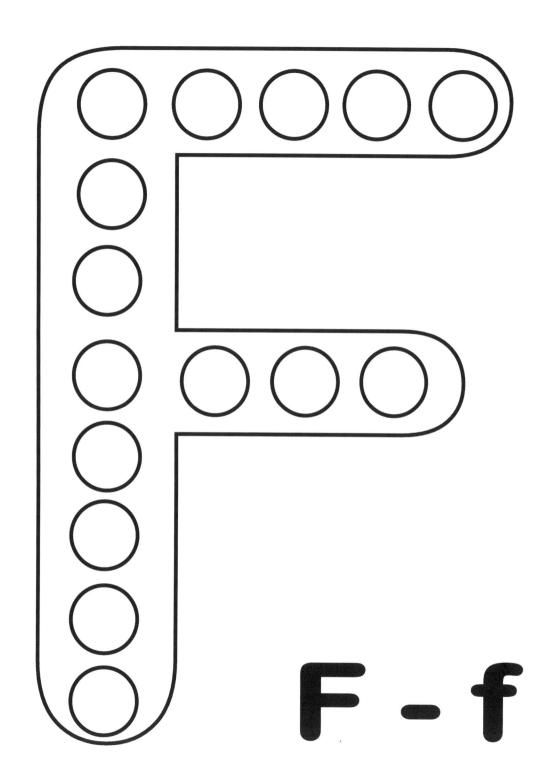

F - f

G - g

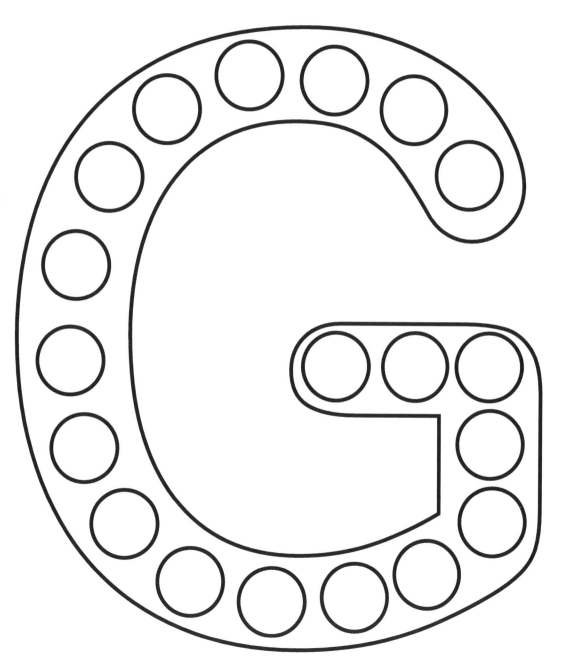

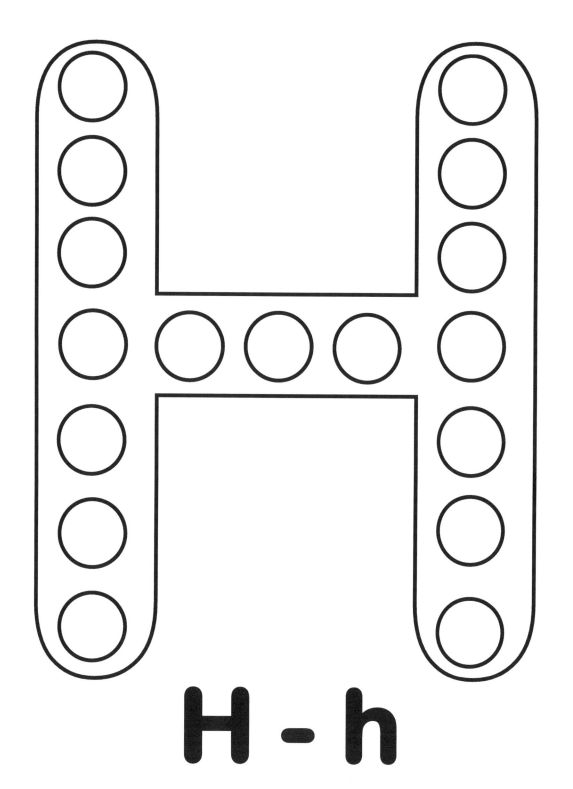

H - h

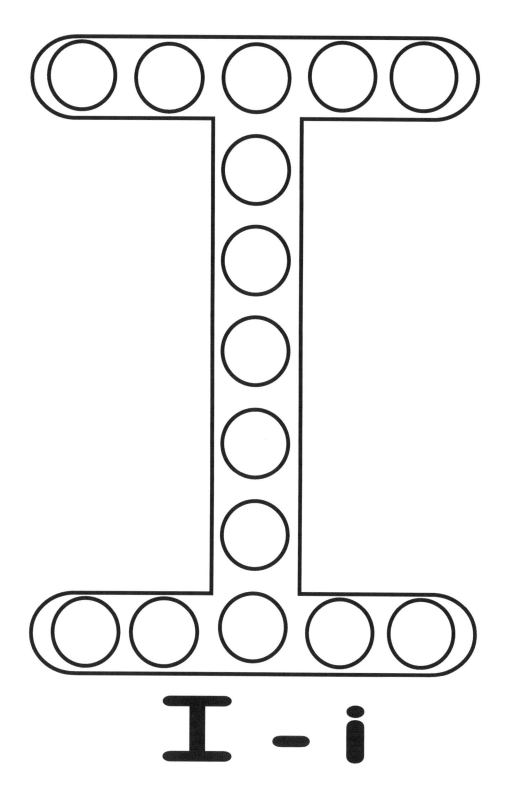

I - i

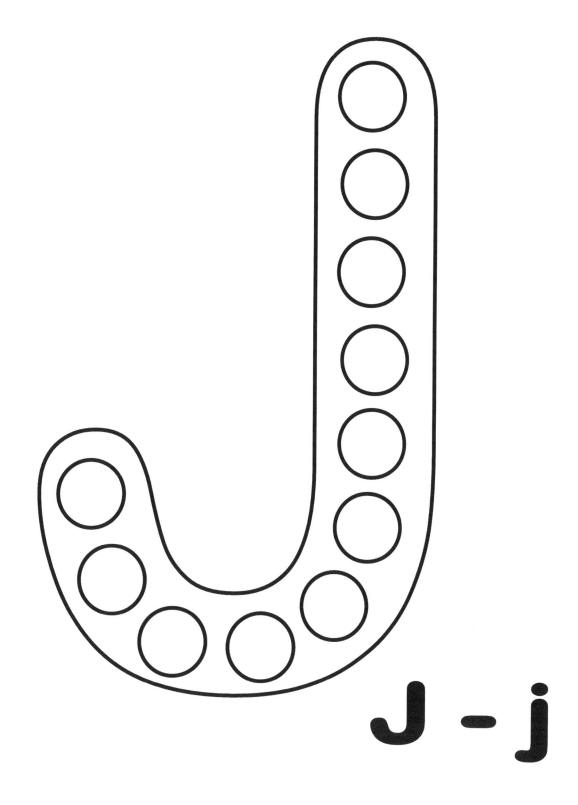

J - j

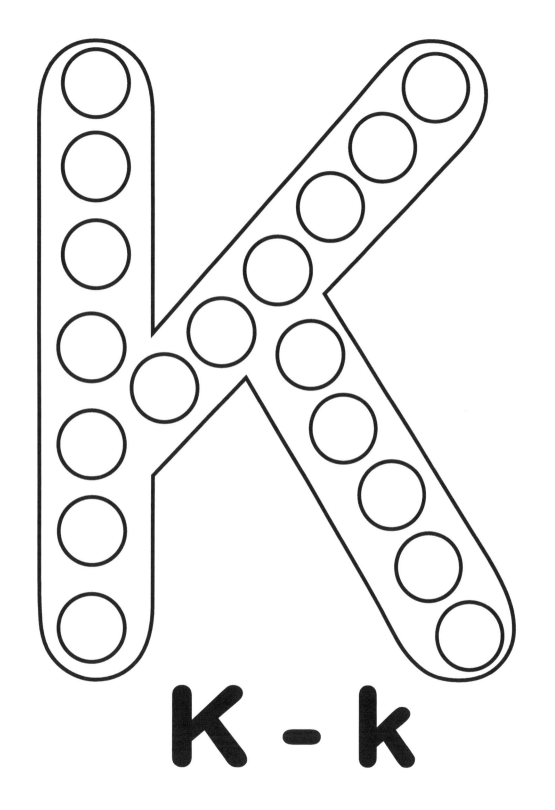

K - k

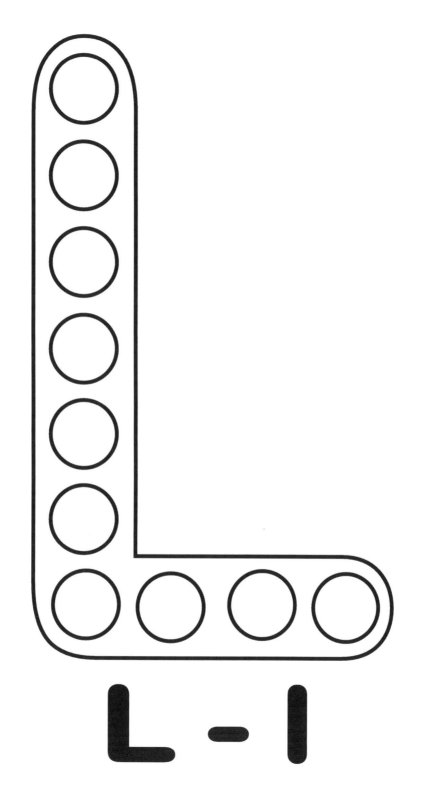

L - l

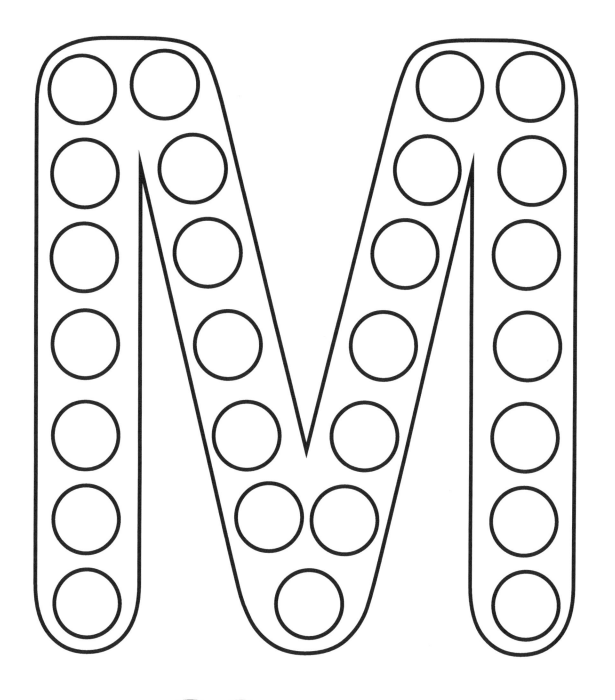

M - m

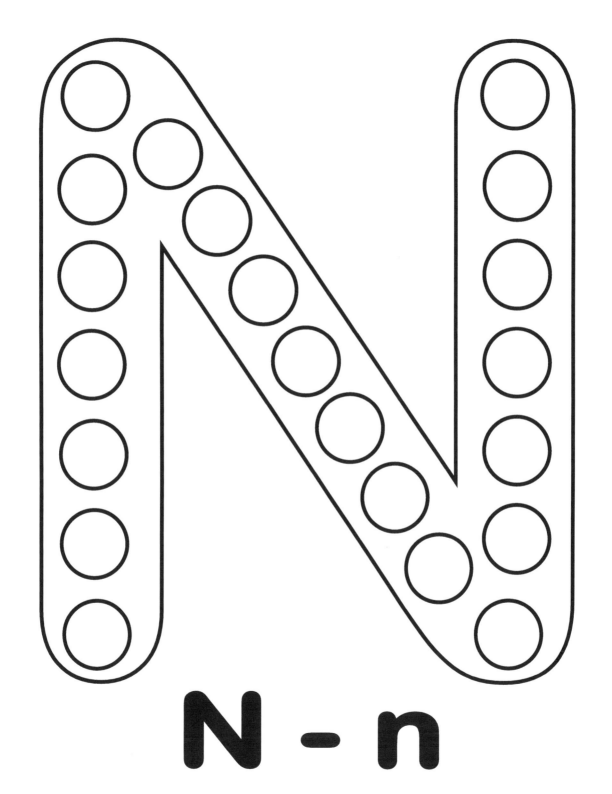

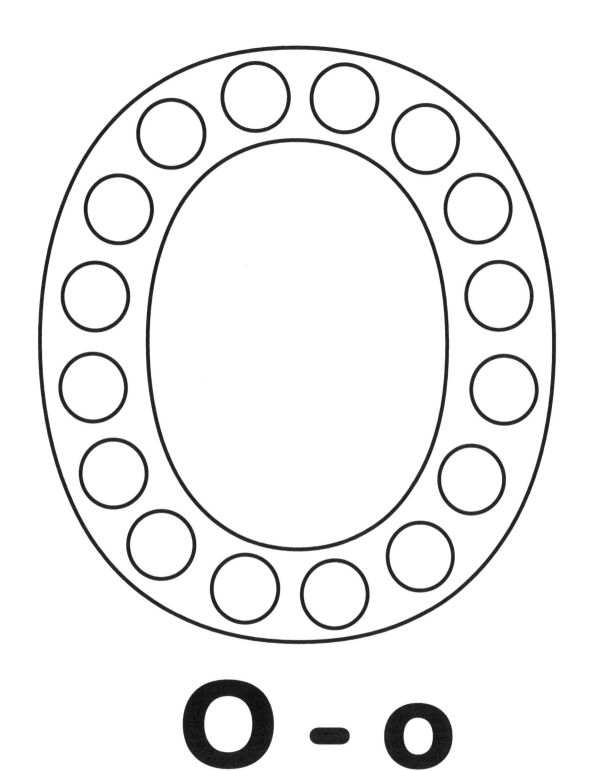

O - o

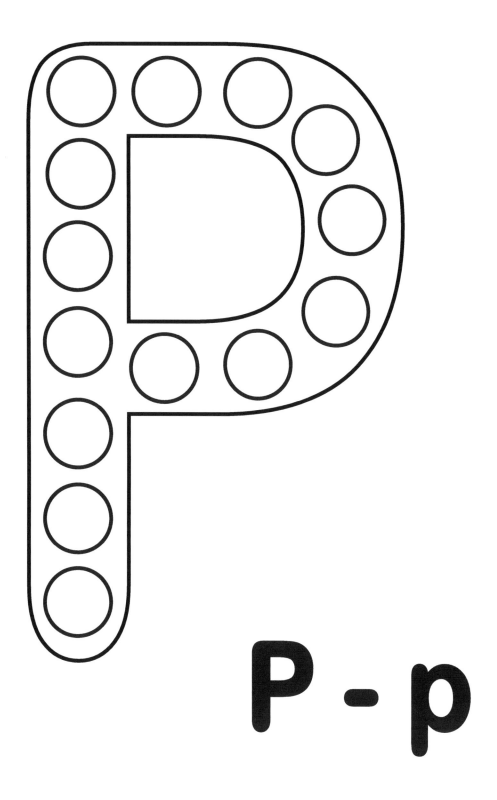

P - p

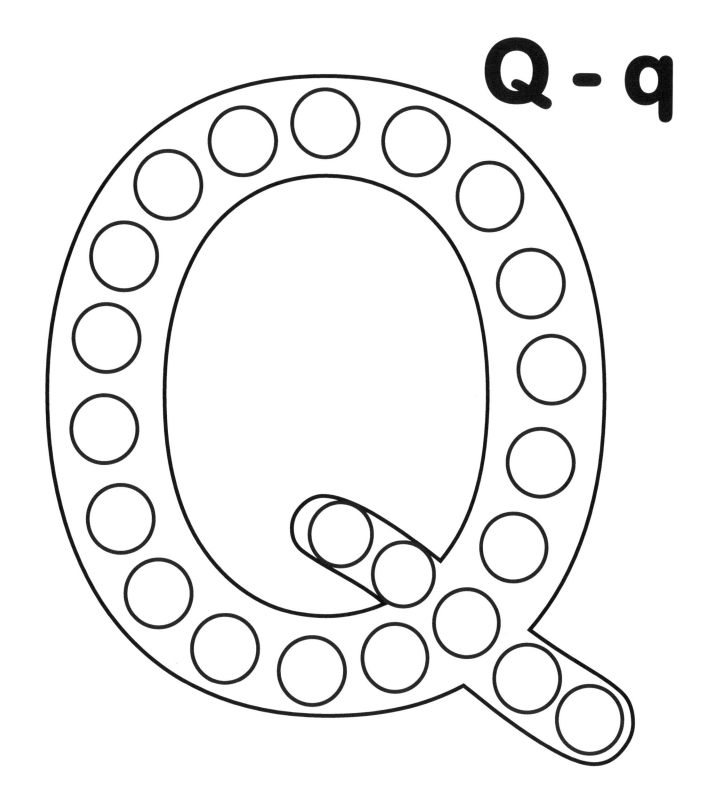

Q - q

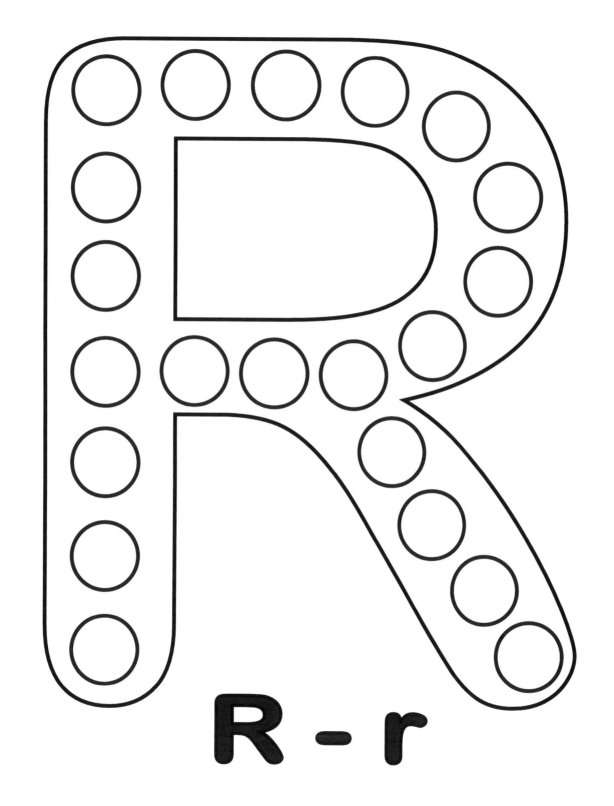

R - r

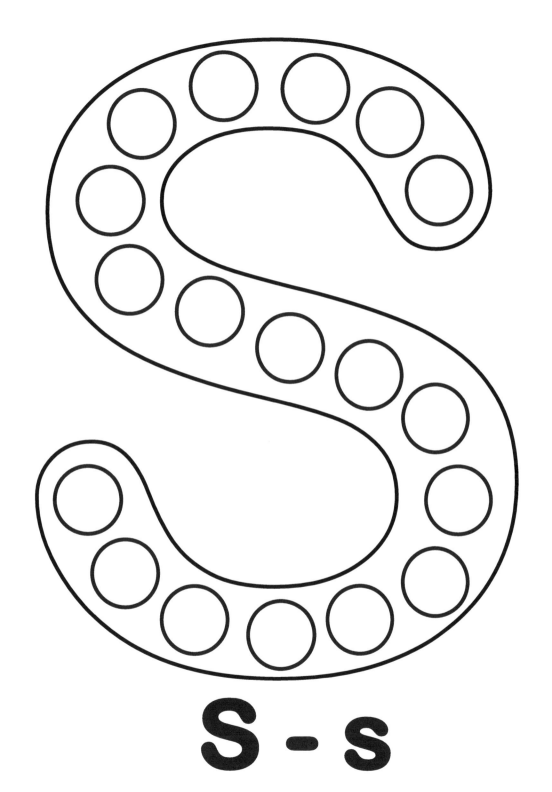

S - s

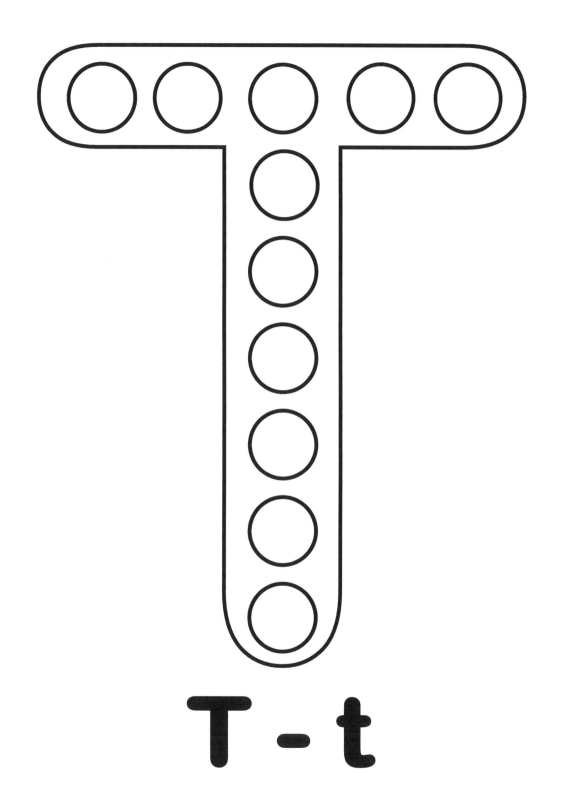

T - t

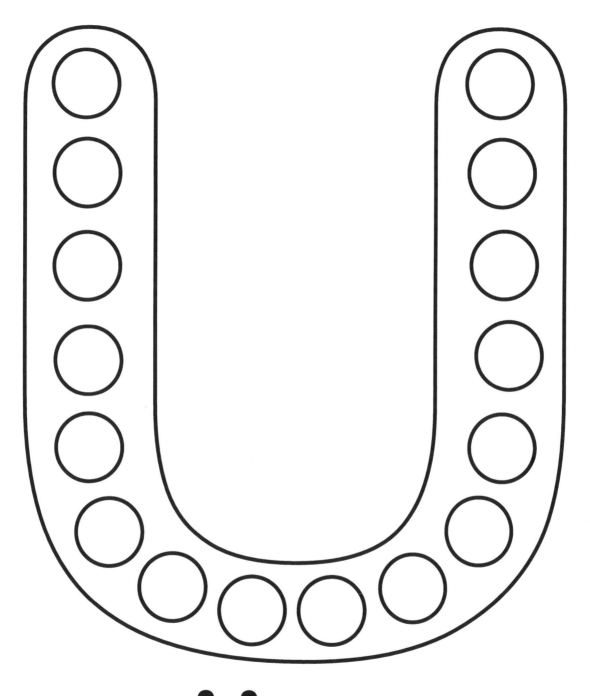

U - u

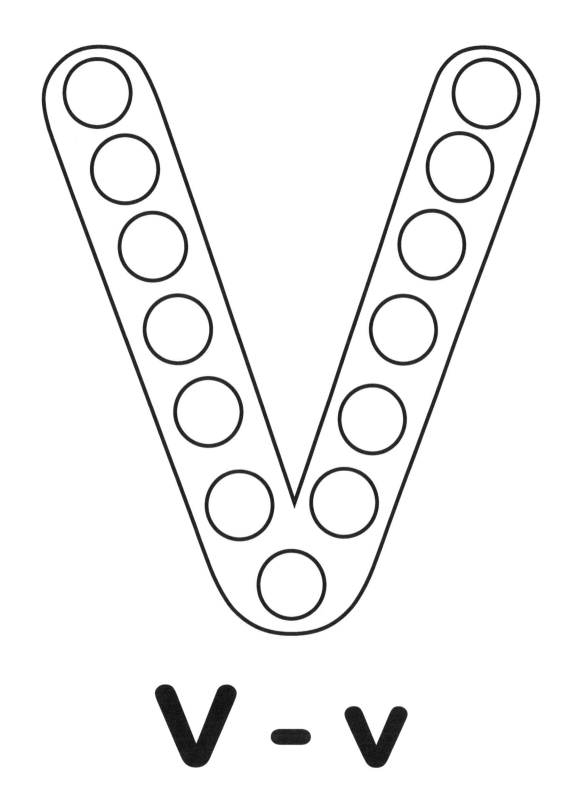

V - v

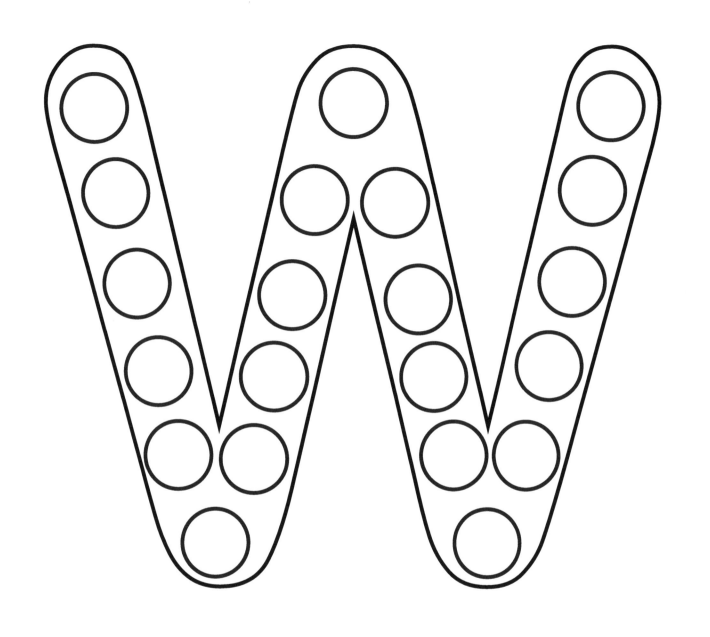

W - w

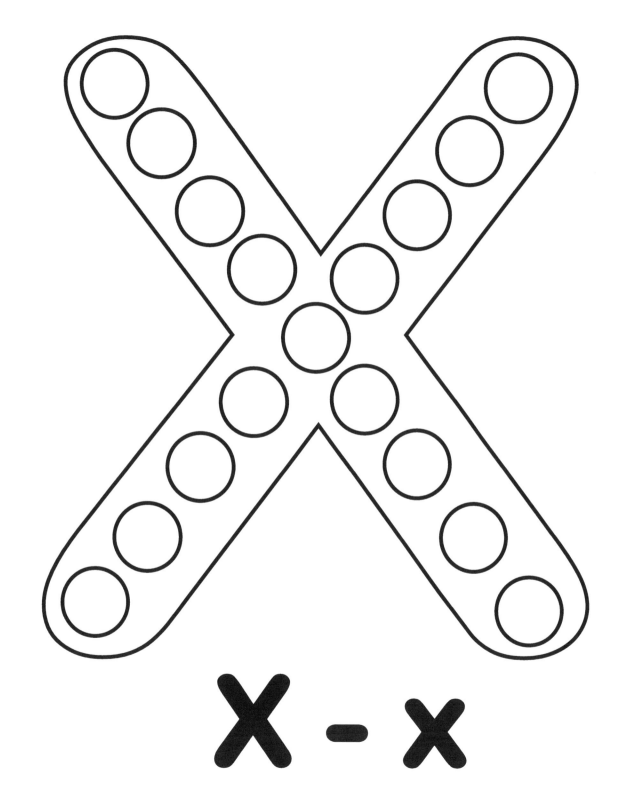

X - x

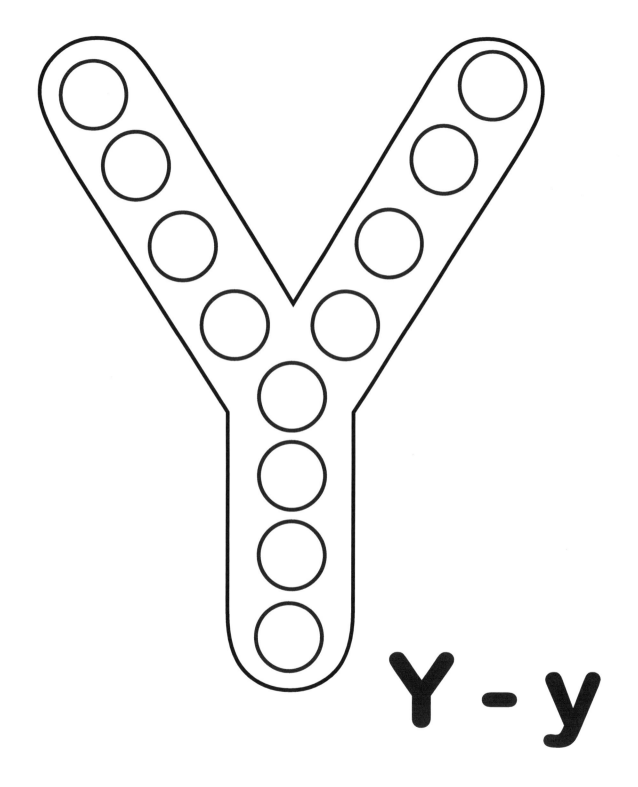

Y - y

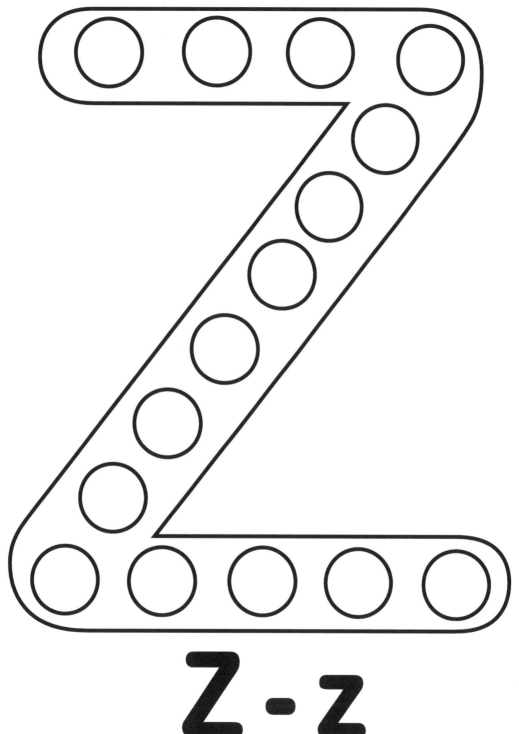

Z - z

Made in the USA
Columbia, SC
03 August 2024

BEYOND the WORMHOLE

CORBIN STRATTON

CREDITS:

Written & Illustrated by: Corbin Stratton

Edited by: Matthew Rice, Tedra Stratton, and Luke Allison

Interior Design & Art Direction by: Jay Ostby

'Cover Design & Art Direction by: Createspace Design Team

FOR DEBRA, ELLA, AND EMILIA

When you think of Christmas elves, what is it that you see?
Are they magic, happy creatures, as joyful as can be?

Are they small and emerald green, with long and pointy ears?
Do they have two big round eyes; are they full of Christmas cheer?

You might notice a resemblance... look hard and you might see...
They look like Aliens from space! Surely you agree?

Aliens from a galaxy far far away.
Fleeing their planet by the universe highway.

This is the story of how they found their true selves.
How Aliens from space became our Christmas Elves.

Our story begins on the frozen planet WISE.
7.2 Light years away from our skies.

The surface of WISE is all ice and snow.
Where temperatures often reach 50 below.

Living on WISE are bright, tiny creatures.
Crafting scientific gadgets with artistic features.

Villages packed with amazing toys and constructions.
The talented elf-folk need no instructions.

Their spirited hearts beat with warmth, love, and glee.
Spending days eating Zocolate and playing games joyfully.

But the elves don't live alone on the planet WISE.
They live under the watch of malevolent eyes.

Hairy yeti that stand nearly 13 feet tall.
With razor sharp teeth most fearsome to all.

They love to hunt elves and each paw can grab two.
Because nothing tastes better than a bowl of elf stew.

Colossal ice castles in which each yeti dwells.
Hold captured elves in laser bar cells.

One captured elf was the great thinker Zark.
Who was caught with his friends at an ice-skating park.

Zark sat in his cell, his mind starting to ponder.
A place past the stars where elves could safely wander.

"If only I wasn't stuck in this place.
We could build a large ship and escape into space."

Zark fell asleep to dream up a plan.
They'd soon all be free, though not by his hand.

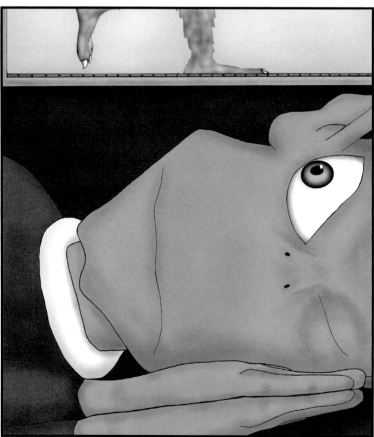

A soft clack in the dark woke Zark from his snooze.
He could hear shuffling feet, but he didn't know whose.

To his great surprise the cell door opened wide.
A friendly yeti, it seemed, was on the elves side.

Up Mount Dag and over icy Lake Gol.
Zark arrived home with a vision to behold.

He gathered the elves into the town square.
To share his idea to improve their welfare.

I'll build a space ship to take us away.
From this land of despair. We'll be happy every day.

From the youngest to oldest they worked from Zark's plan.
Building all night and day, every woman and man.

They worked 40 days through the 40th night.
Til the spaceship was finished and ready for flight.

The spaceship was a true wonder to see.
As big as a stadium and red like a ruby.

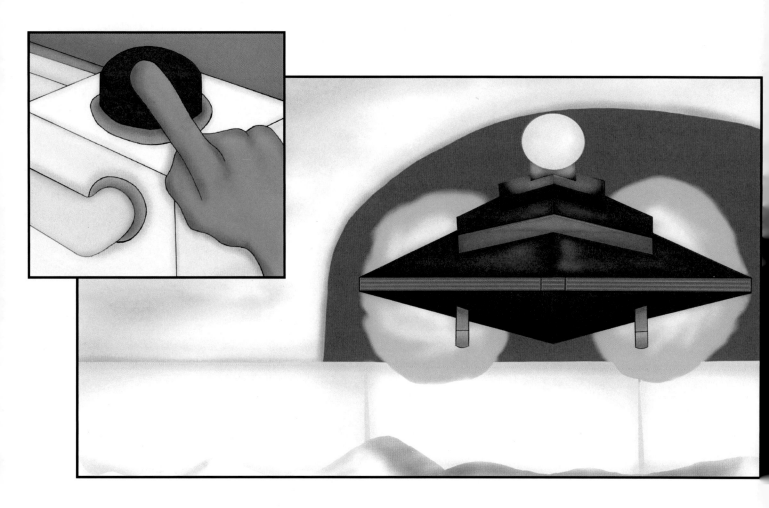

Everyone packed up and boarded the ship.
Zark plotted a course for the very long trip.

With a push of a button the ship came alive.
Flames burst from the back as Zark engaged hyperdrive.

The ship skated on snow then shot to the sky.
And after leaving the planet all the elves said goodbye.

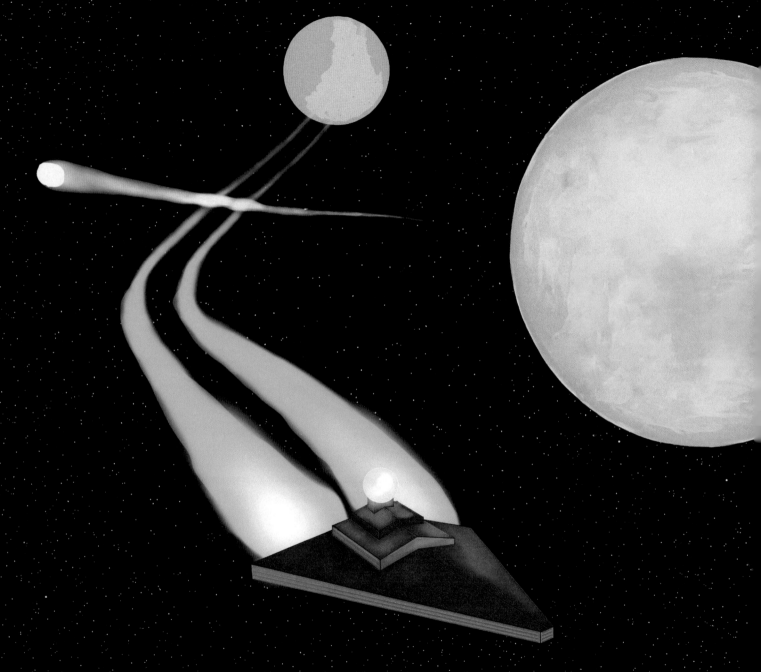

Over the moon and through a comet's tail.
They flew past a nearby planet and continued to sail.

The ship finally arrived at a spiraling white light.
At its center a blue-green planet was in sight.

Into the wormhole the Elves bravely flew.
Instantly transported from the old galaxy to the new.

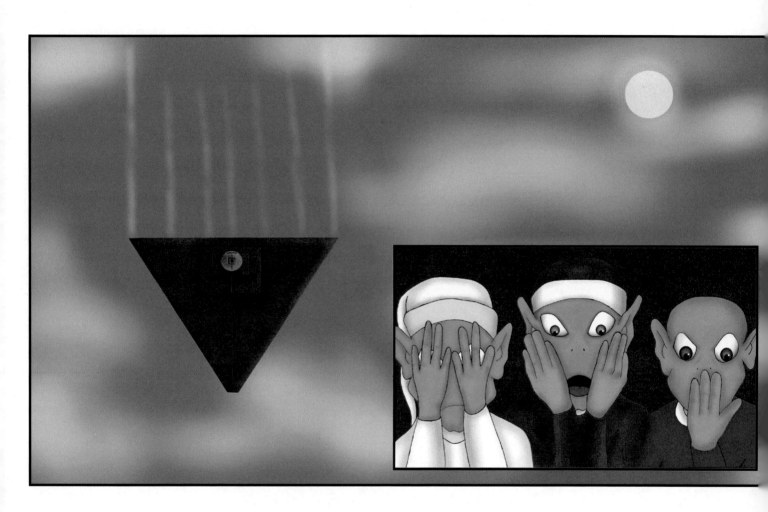

Crossing into our galaxy drained the ship of its power.
All the elves could do now was hold on and cower.

The ship was caught in Earth's gravitational pull.
Plummeting down with no hope of control.

A river named Myros cushioned their fall.
The crash causing a wave over 50 feet tall.

Zark climbed from the ship not knowing where they could be.
They had crashed in Lycia in year 342 AD.

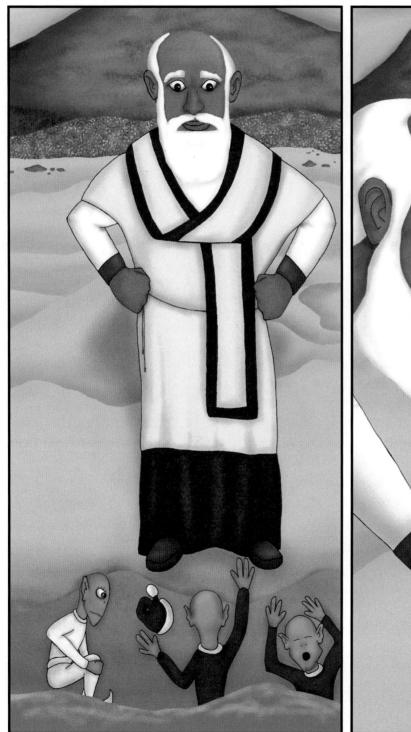

They collapsed on the beach after swimming to the shore.
Their bodies were weary, battered, and sore.
They needed some help and they needed it quick,
When along came a bishop by the name of Saint Nick.

He had a white beard, but not a hair on his head.
His long, flowing robes were colored white and red.
"Wherever you came from, you clearly need a bed,
So come stay at my cathedral," Nicolas said.

With a shake of the hand Zark agreed to Nick's plan.
All the elves had a bed, every child, woman, and man.

Nicholas nursed them all back to health
So the elves helped bring gifts to the kids without wealth.

The elves loved giving gifts to the girls and the boys
So they turned their talents to making new toys.

An idea came to Zark like a beacon of light.
"We should give gifts to all kids every year on this night!"

If the elves built the toys and loaded their ship
They could deliver it all at a supersonic clip!

Nick loved this plan, "But we need lots more space."
"I'll come join you later once you find a home base."

The elves towed their ship from the river to shore.
After drying it out they could blast off once more.

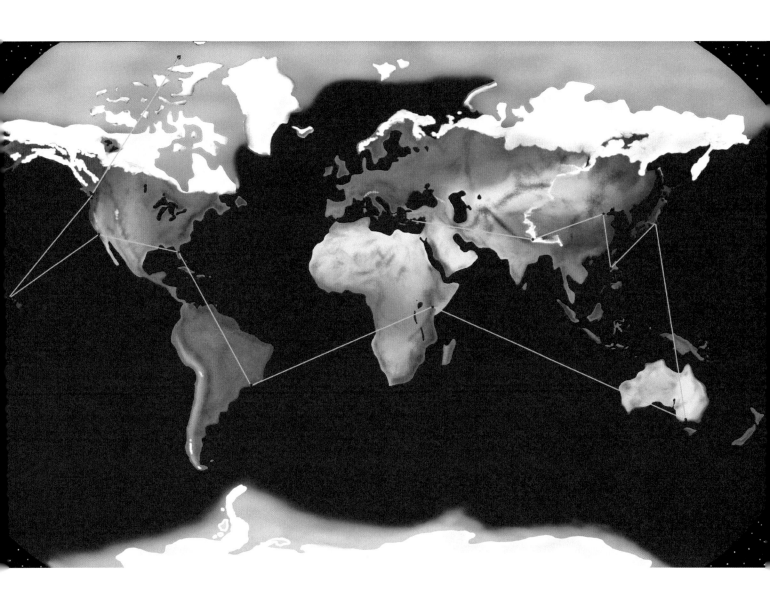

They zoomed around Earth from the east to the west.
Searching for land that would suit them the best.

When they came to the Arctic way up in the north.
They discovered a spot they could live in henceforth.

It was frozen like WISE but without abominable beasts.
So they planted the North Pole and held a mighty feast.

The great frozen north would be their new land.
This was working out better than even Zark planned.

On Christmas Eve when you look to the sky.
Who is it you see high above flying by?

Someone brings gifts to put under your tree.
But who would do that? Who could it be?

Is it a bird? Is it a plane? Is it a hero in tights?
Or eight magic reindeer lead by a nose shining bright?

Those ideas all sound fine, but if you've listened to me,
you know its Saint Nick and the space elf colony.
Bringing gifts, spreading joy, and good old Christmas Glee.

The end...

Made in the USA
San Bernardino, CA
28 June 2020